Bereavement

A Guide to understanding and coping with
your grief

Table of Contents

Introduction

What are the key aspects of grief?

The death of someone close to us often presents a voyage through some of the most challenging and intense emotions that we may ever have to face. The prospect of having to adjust to life without your loved one can at times seem inconceivable, and the daunting journey of recovery like an enormous mountain to climb. However, despite the rollercoaster of feelings that we encounter, and the fear that we ourselves will never quite be the same again, the distress caused by grieving is something that can be reduced by being understood, and shared.

Most people would agree that being human is a complicated enough business already, without the loss of a loved one coming along to shake up our world. The sheer mental – and sometimes physical – pain that we endure after bereavement can be unlike anything else we have experienced, and it is paramount that we treat ourselves delicately, and take time to reflect on our feelings and emotional state. But it is not always easy to know when to allow yourself to indulge a little in your sorrow, and when to force yourself to be more active. Being somewhat analytical and reflective can help you identify these key moments in your grief.

Grief can be defined as a normal and natural reaction to loss, and has aspects that are both universal, as well as extremely personal. Directly after the passing away of your loved one, you may experience emotions that you perhaps expected, such as a powerful sense of sadness and sorrow, and yearning for your lost one. However, bereavement can also give rise to other more complicated feelings, such as anger, disbelief, and guilt, all of which we will consider in the following chapters.

Is recovery just a waiting game?

Time is often the remedy prescribed for a broken heart or any sort of loss, and seen as the main factor in the healing process. Indeed, it is likely that it will take a considerable length of time for grieving to run its course, and can be vastly different for everyone, from a few months to some years. As time passes, different emotions may become prevalent and others can fade away; eventually the grief itself moves from the forefront slowly to the back of your mind. But must we remain passive to all these intense sensations while time ticks along? Although death, and grief, are an unavoidable part of life, most people would agree that there is no quick and easy cure for it, and that grief and sorrow are things that only time can heal. Current research, however, has shown that seeking support and remaining pro-active in the process can greatly help reduce the negativity of the experience, such as depression, and ease the resolution of grieving and the acceptance of a new life. Throughout, it is important to be in touch with how you are feeling, to be active in the storm of emotions, rather than being tossed about at sea.

What are the aims of this book?

Your story, in terms of your loved one and what they meant to you when living, and how you feel now that they are gone, is unique. Your grief is also unique, and the way in which you will experience the grieving process will be entirely personal to you. But that is not to say that you shouldn't try and share your thoughts and feelings; it will perhaps be lonely at times, but it need not be a solitary journey.

Our goal is to help readers achieve a peaceful acceptance of their loss as fully and healthily as possible, while attempting to limit the swathe of negative feelings that may be engulfing you. As such this book will try to guide you through the main emotions that are associated with grief, and try to make you aware of some tools that can help you deal with each emotional state that you may encounter along the way. We will consider what theories are out there that can help us try to understand the grieving process, and also look at some recent examples of how people have tackled and shared their grief.

Chapter 1
The emotional stages – or states – of grief

The stage model of grief

Many books or pamphlets that you might come across give reference to a five or seven stage model of grieving. This is based on the work of psychiatrist Elisabeth Kübler-Ross who wrote an influential book called 'On Death and Dying' in 1969 (1), in which she identified five distinct emotional stages that a grieving person may experience: denial – anger – bargaining – depression – acceptance. The idea was that there were clear stages through the grieving process, separate from the others, although the stages could happen in any order and some people may not even experience one at all (e.g. some people never experience denial that their love one is dead, whereas others will spend a long time grasping with the reality of their loss). Even though Kübler-Ross's book was written mostly from the perspective of dying person's feelings rather than the survivor's feelings, the emotions identified, and the idea that grieving was a journey characterised by stages, has meant that it has remained a hugely popular and understandable reference for those dealing with loss. In later years, other researchers have refined and reworked the model, often adding emotions such as shock/disbelief and guilt, resulting in a seven-stage model.

States of grief

A more current idea, based on studies of the actual experience of the grieving person, is that while the five (or seven) stage model does identify relevant emotions, they are better described to occur in a variety of emotional states rather than precise stages. (2) Although the grieving process can be very much like a journey, emotions can come, go, and reappear again at any time without any linear path, so the notion of passing to a new stage and closing the door on the previous one is perhaps not really accurate or helpful. One proponent of this idea is self-help author Dr Natasha Josefowitz, who questioned recently bereaved people about their grief and wrote about the '7 Emotional States of Loss' (3) which she had identified in their experiences. She wrote the following interesting observation about the states of grief:

"Although I have attempted to categorise these in some sort of sequence, not all people went through these emotional states nor did they all encounter them in the order I propose. At times, many reverted to a previously experienced state before moving on. These emotional states, painful as they feel, are the stepping-stones to healing".

Although a valuable insight, Josefowitz's research focused only on elderly people who had lost their spouses, hence their experiences are likely to be very similar to one another's and not perhaps as similar to those of younger people or those dealing with the loss of a parent, friend or child. So while it is interesting to read her perspective, here we have looked at the wider picture and tried to draw together as many useful observations and ideas as we can.

This book will focus on the idea of states of grief, and will offer practical tools and examples of dealing with the key emotions which might be predominant at different times. Although the states are written here in an order, it is very important to bear in mind that your experience may be entirely different, and although there are common themes and experiences in bereavement, there is certainly no set path through the process.

The main thing is knowing that you and your resilience are at the centre of the story, and that the resolution of your grief – and the acceptance of your new life as a survivor – is within your reach.

Chapter 2
Shock, denial and disbelief

Initial reaction to the death of a loved one

Even when the death of a loved one has been long expected, such as due to an illness or to old age, when it finally occurs, the initial reaction can be one of absolute shock that they are truly gone. Many people find that they are numb; some even say it is like a paralysis where they can't think or move for a short time. There can also be a strong physical reaction, such as fainting, becoming pale or having a shortness of breath. Because of this, it is very important to sit down somewhere private and quiet and have people around you at this point.

Sometimes the shock can be even more powerful when the death is sudden and wholly unexpected, and the survivors struggle intensely to believe that it is true, or hold onto hope that there must be a mistake somewhere, particularly if they have never had the chance to see them one last time or to say goodbye. These feelings of disbelief and denial can be very common as part of the initial shock, but usually wear off fairly quickly as the unfortunate reality begins to set in.

A sense of numbness may cushion the initial blow of the loss, which some people find helpful to make them function through the initial hub of activity, such as making funeral arrangements and calling friends and family to tell them the news. As you say the words that the person has died, you still might find it incredible, and remain in disbelief that what you are saying is true.

The overriding feeling of shock and numbness, before other feelings – such as sadness and longing – take over, and can last for a very short period of time, maybe mere minutes for some, days or weeks for others. Some people may not feel any shock at all, and accept from the very start that their loved one is gone. It is a very different experience for everyone.

The initial state of shock and disbelief can be so intense that it would be easy to think that once it eases off, that it has gone. But in some ways a sense of disbelief can last much longer in terms of your natural reflexes, as your mind and senses reprogramme themselves to life without that person. For example, for a split second you may think you see them on a busy street, or that it is their key turning in the door, or when the phone rings, it's them. These can be very painful moments when you forget for a moment that they are gone, and each time you have to teach yourself to think again, and gradually modify your habits.

Example

Although a sense of disbelief is understandable in the hours and days following the news of a death, denying that the death occurred for an extended period can stall the grieving process and delay the eventual acceptance that your loved one has gone.

Try to deal and not to be evasive when asked any questions that remind you of your bereavement. You might find it extremely hard to explain that he/she is dead, but the more you get used to saying it, and talking about them, the better for your understanding and eventual acceptance. You may also find that by bringing them into conversation with other people, you keep their memory alive and relevant in your day-to-day life, rather than hidden away.

If you recognise yourself being in continued denial, you may find yourself hiding away from any reminders of the person who is missing in your life. It is best not to shy away from certain dates or places, but rather try to find a way to celebrate them in a personal and gentle way (i.e. you don't need to throw a big party, but try to celebrate birthdays or anniversaries in a way that you think they would have enjoyed, such as ordering their favourite food or retracing a walk that you used to share, lighting a sky lantern with a written message on it, or planting a tree in their memory).

Key points to remember

- Even if you might be prepared for the event of a death, it can still come as a strong shock, affecting you both mentally and physically.
- It is important not to be alone at this time and to allow the news to sink in.
- Although the initial intensity of shock may pass quickly, a sense of disbelief can last much longer in terms of having to reprogramme your natural reflexes and expectations of seeing that person in day-to-day life.
- Remaining in denial for an extended period may complicate your eventual progression through the grief and your acceptance of the loss.
- Try to celebrate the person and not avoid reminders that they are gone.

Chapter 3
Pain & yearning

Pain & yearning

As the days go by and the shock subsides, you may really start to comprehend that the special person is now gone. It can seem that your life now has an enormous hole where they once were, and a distressing and powerful sense of yearning may now set in. Yearning is often defined as the strong desire to have someone back as part of your life, and is a feeling that can extend throughout the entire grieving process. It can also be a very unpredictable sensation. A 'good' day, where you have been able to go about and enjoy a relatively normal life, and feel that you are adjusting well, can suddenly give way to a 'bad' day, where missing the person is almost unbearable and stops any feeling of happiness or the participation in activities. Similarly, some days, being reminded of the person can be welcome, and you can be happy to talk of them for a while, and other days it may cause you intense anguish. It is likely that yearning may be the predominant emotion that you feel throughout your grief, and perhaps in some form for many years after.

Together with yearning can come feelings of pain, sometimes a real physical ache, and longing for the person. It can be very hard to express these feelings to friends or family, because the emotions are often very consuming and hard to describe. But it is good to persist in trying, even if you worry that you are bothering people or bringing them down. More often, people are willing to help and try to understand how you are feeling, but they don't always know how to start a conversation about your grief, or fear that they are reminding you of it.

When the longing has lessened and is more bearable, never feel guilty for smiling in a moment's happiness or distraction. You need to look after yourself and allow yourself to find breaks in the grieving process whenever you can. Eventually the pain and yearning will lift and fade, and you can adjust to life without the person, knowing that it does not mean losing them from your thoughts.

Example

The intense yearning or pining for someone can prevent you from being able to see or construct a future without them. Although missing someone is absolutely natural and will perhaps always be present in some form, when you find that you lose interest in eating, participating in any activities, or looking after yourself, then it has become a problem.

If you feel consumed with thoughts of your loved one and the belief that your life is incomplete without them, it can help to set a series of goals for yourself to help find a pathway out of the hold that the yearning has over you, step by step. Of course you can start with smaller ideas to take your mind off your grief for a moment, such as watching a funny TV programme or an interesting film. You may be scared of letting go of your grief for a moment, after all, in some ways, the intensity of grieving can make you feel that it is keeping you close and connected with your loved one. But even if it seems like an effort, now is the time to be a little hard on yourself and force yourself to give it a try, otherwise you risk being stuck in a passive period of longing which, as time goes on, may impede your progress and make it harder to start the gradual adjustment to rebuilding your life.

As you manage the first step, see how you felt before and after. Were you able to become distracted for a moment, and be taken away from your grief? How did it feel to return to thoughts of your loved one afterwards? Or were you unable to concentrate on the programme at all? Or have you tried to focus but everything seemed to remind you of your loss? All these difficult reactions are understandable, but you should not be deterred from trying again, as the next time your response could be completely different.

With each small step, you may have the confidence to build up and set targets week by week: see a film this week, visit an old friend the next. Some people use the analogy of stepping-stones, making one small step just to reach the next. Before you know it, you may have travelled a good distance. Make the plans that feel right in order to take a small step, and help you to keep active without overly challenging yourself.

Key points to remember

- Pain and yearning are some of the most distressing emotions in the grieving process, and represent the intensity of the loss that you feel.
- Missing your loved one can become so consuming that it prevents you from beginning to reconstruct or carry on your life without them.
- Making some goals for yourself that are realistic and flexible, with the aim of keeping you social and active, will be very helpful in the eventual resolution of your grief.

Chapter 4
Anger, bargaining
& guilt

Experiences of anger and guilt

Although some people might not experience any anger at all in bereavement, for those who do, it can be a very difficult emotion to reckon with. Anger can arise from the pain of your loss, as well as the frustrating and unwanted hurdles that you may encounter in your grief. The questions of 'why do I have to deal with this alone?' or 'why must I be sad? I deserve to be happy!' are just a couple of examples of the frustrations that can lead to anger. Anger can also arise from the anguishing questions of 'what-if?' Such as: 'What if a different doctor had been able to save him/her?' 'What if we hadn't gone there?' 'What if we had taken better care of each other?' The resulting anger may be directed at someone specific, for example the medical staff who weren't able to save the person, someone who caused an accident, or someone very close to you, such as a family member. In many cases where the deceased person is perceived to have contributed in some way to their death through their lifestyle such as risk taking, not looking after themselves, drug abuse, or perhaps even if they committed suicide, a common reaction is a sense of anger towards that person, much as you may love and miss them still. Similarly, and often intertwined, can be a sense of guilt and anger with yourself, and questioning 'why didn't I say this or do this more?' or 'how could I have let this happen?' For many mourners, the resentment might just be directed at the whole world in general for refusing to stand still or take notice when your whole life has changed.

The sense of anger can be manifested in different ways throughout the grieving process and may vary depending on individual experience. For example, some people may be able to verbalise their angry feelings and identify the root of the frustration through sharing their thoughts. Others find it very hard to talk honestly about their struggles and the anger can bubble up in intense rages that are violent and hard to manage. Apart from talking and sharing the thoughts before they manifest in a rage, anger can also be channelled into positive energy, for example sports and keeping fit, or being busy with work or voluntary activities. For some, introspective activities such as meditation can help dissipate the angry energy, rather than transferring it into something else. The important factor is not ignoring it or letting it build up and become unmanageable, because uncontrolled rage can destroy your precious social networks or hurt those close to you.

If you are someone who has never really experienced anger before in your life, it can be an extremely difficult thing to deal with, and you may fear that your own nature has changed. Who is this person who flies into a rage at the smallest thing, is suddenly jealous of their friends and bitter with the world at large? The important thing to remember is that it is an entirely normal response to bereavement, and that with the right management, you will be able to reason with and manage the anger, and that one day it should be behind you for good.

Bargaining and religion

Throughout the grieving process, there is of course a heightened sense of the meaning of life and an awareness of the finality and proximity of death. So it follows that such a significant and life changing event as bereavement can have repercussions on religious beliefs for many people as they seek to resolve the question of 'why?' Those who held religious beliefs may now question why God would not listen to their prayers, or why God did not save their loved one, and harbour anger and blame towards God for allowing such a devastating loss to happen to them. Conversely, those who were not religious may now seek out comfort in the thought of an afterlife or a spiritual meaning to life and death, to try and make sense of their experience. There may be some comfort to be found in the idea that life is eternal, and in death they will be reunited with their loved ones who have passed away. Having a relationship with whatever perceived higher power may lead to a period of bargaining and pleading for the current state of affairs to be changed, to please bring back your loved one in return for giving up sinful ways and becoming a model Christian or Muslim, for example. It is a desperate but understandable hope for the unfortunate events to be reversed and to continue living your life as you had done before.

Example

Anger is a sensation that can be very difficult to manage and keep under physical control. Avoiding it or failing to resolve where it comes from can lead to lashing out, and in turn lead to more problems and chaos in our lives. Unresolved anger and blame may contribute to marriages breaking up, and families becoming alienated from one another after a loss. It is vital to try and deal with all this negative energy before it damages your support networks, as it is those that you need to reply upon to assist you through your grief.

There can be a two-pronged approach to dealing with anger and resentment. Firstly, deal with anger and the negative energy created by it by being active. This means you could exercise or participate in sports, sing at the top of your lungs, or throw yourself into a new project. You can also try breathing techniques to expel all the negativity out of your body, visualising all the anger leaving you with each deep breath. These ideas can help to channel the emotion out from your mind and body and convert it into positive output. Secondly, by analysing the angry feelings, either at the time, or shortly afterwards when you feel calmer, you may be able to learn what caused it and this should help you verbalise and reason with it. For example, a friend invites you to dinner and accidentally pours wine over you, spoiling your outfit. You experience a flash of anger and annoyance, which you struggle to control. You can rationalise that it was just an accident, but your anger may remain somewhat out of proportion to how you might have reacted previous to the bereavement. Instead of shouting at your friend, you may need to take some deep breaths or excuse yourself to have a moment of fresh air to release the angry energy, and then once you can think clearly you can analyse why it upset you so much. Perhaps however insignificant, it is just another episode of bad luck to happen and you feel sorry for yourself, or it is because you are reminded that your partner is no longer there to laugh a silly accident off with. If you prepare yourself to deal with anger when it comes, and examine it afterwards, this should help to reduce further instances and make it much more likely that you won't lash out or become resentful of those closest to you.

As hard as anger can be to manage, being often anti-social, challenging and sometimes downright ugly, it has to be dealt with head on rather than suppressed.

Key points to remember

- Experiences of anger and guilt are common in grief, and can be manifestations of how much you miss the person in your life and appreciate what they meant to you when alive.

- As anger can cause unpleasant situations with friends, family and in society, there may be temptation to hide it away and not try and share your emotions.
- Some people direct anger towards God for letting bad things happen to them, and many find that their sense of religion, spirituality and outlook on the meaning of life can be changed by bereavement.
- It is essential to deal with negative energy by being active rather than repressing it, and also analysing what caused it, to try and help reduce further angry outbreaks.

Chapter 5
Depression

Depression after bereavement

Depression can be broadly defined as feelings of melancholy and disinterest, and some degree of depression is seen as a normal part of the grieving process. These periods are typified by feelings of being low and passive, together with other characteristics such as a lack of concentration and insomnia. You may lose the will to do anything, and feel unable to take pleasure in any activities, even finding that you have lost interest in eating and drinking. You just want to be left alone to mourn and cry and shy away from any social interaction whatsoever. Any anger you may have had seems to have dissipated, or perhaps has been turned inwards on yourself, along with feelings of guilt and regret. This cloud of depression can be entangled with the sense of yearning you have for your loved one, and the recognition that they are not coming back. Your mind is turned inwards, and you are consumed with gloomy thoughts.

Studies show that feelings of depression peak at around 6 months after losing someone (4) though – as with all other aspects of grieving – there is no set rule for everybody. Some may fall into a period of depression immediately after the death of their loved one which may either lift quickly or take much longer to pass, and others will experience the negative emotions after bereavement, such as sadness and longing, but without any characteristics of depression.

It is often thought that there are gender differences in expressing negative emotions such as depression. Women are seen as being much more able to verbalise and talk through their emotions – even uncomfortable ones – with friends, co-workers, family, and strangers. Some research has indicated that when it comes to the death of a child, women tended to grieve more openly than men, and made more use of support groups, and were also found to function better on a day-to-day basis, perhaps inclined to keep going and hold the family together (5). In this way, women were found to have more coping strategies than men, who were less likely to express emotions, and therefore it is men who may more commonly end up with undiagnosed depression issues because they hide their feelings away.

Whether male or female, young or old, the key to getting through depressive periods, whenever they descend upon you, is to keep people around you, and not feel afraid to talk about your feelings. If your support networks are not non-judgemental enough or don't have adequate listeners, or you don't feel able to share your struggles with depression with people you know, there are also many specialised helplines to call, which we will refer to in the later chapter, "When to Seek Help for Unresolved Grief."

Example

As depression can overcome us like a gloomy fog full of despondent feelings and resigned thoughts, it can be extremely difficult to shake off. You may be feeling exhausted already after months of intense grieving, and fear that you will never resolve the negative and distressing emotions inside in order to construct a new life. Perhaps fed up with feeling low, you have stopped sharing your emotions with friends and family, or you think that you are becoming a burden and bringing them down. How can you think or act your way out of it?

Feeling passive and depressed is a hard state to break out of, once it gets its claws into you, and you can be easily defeated in any attempt you might make. Over time, this can lead to you bothering less with social networks and risking these falling away, which can lead to you becoming even further demoralised. To help break the cycle of depressive thoughts, there is a type of therapy called cognitive behavioural therapy (CBT), which can offer some useful techniques to be used by yourself at home. Essentially, the idea behind CBT is to help manage your emotional state by questioning and trying to influence it, and by realising just how much your thoughts, feelings and behaviour are very closely related. The goal of CBT is to be able to think yourself better, through replacing negative thoughts with positive thoughts and actions. Before you know it, your feelings will become a little more positive too.

So in practice how would this work?

First of all, you must try to recognise when you are thinking depressive thoughts. For example: "There's no point in cooking dinner, now that I'm on my own" or "I won't enjoy socialising, so there's no point in going out." Once you have identified these, try and question them or reason with them. "Well, my health is still important and I still need to eat," or "who knows what will happen? I may enjoy myself and it might be nice to get out for once." Ask yourself: what would a friend or family member be doing in your shoes? Would they behave differently? What if you try and change your behaviour for once and cook yourself a nice dinner, or go out and socialise? How would that make you feel? Step by step, you may be able to get yourself to be flexible in your thinking and make it less likely that a cycle of negative and defeated thoughts will keep your mood down for long.

Physical exercise can make a huge impact on a state of depression, as it stimulates the body to produce endorphins, which are the body's natural painkillers and anti-depressants. Of course, if you are feeling depressed, it can be extremely difficult to get motivated to do anything, so start small. If you don't want to leave home, begin with some stretches or gentle yoga movements (you can watch thousands of YouTube videos to get you started). If you are a gardener, getting out and about in the garden can be very positive exercise, and also will help you receive natural sunlight which is hugely beneficial to your health and mood. Once you feel bolder, you may choose to take a walk or a gentle run, or find something fun to do at the local gym, or go for a swim.

There is no easy way out of depressive feelings when they are upon you, but keeping your negative thoughts in check, and trying to keep active, can really help ease off the worst of it, and give you the tools you need to help you along in your recovery.

Key points to remember

- Depression in some form is a normal part of the grieving process, and is typified by a lack of motivation to do anything, and a gloomy mood taking away any experience of pleasure.
- Men and women may feel able to express depression differently, and their experiences of it may be different. With everyone, keeping a support network around you is fundamental.
- Cognitive or 'thinking' self-help techniques can be useful to stop a cycle of depression by trying to replace negative thoughts with positive ones.
- Incorporating some mild physical exercise into your day can really help ease off the depression and allow you to move towards resolving your grief.

Chapter 6
Acceptance, and the 'new normal'

What is the 'new normal?'

It is hard to pinpoint the exact moment when things start looking up, and you find that you are being able to slowly reconstruct your life and put energy into a new future. Your loved one may still be an ongoing presence in your thoughts, but the sadness, anger and longing have lifted enough for you to be able to think of them and refer to them without the anguish and almost paralysing yearning that you might once have had. So how did you get here? Was it just a matter of time? In retrospect, you can look at everything you have been through in the past weeks and months, and see that all the emotions and trials that you have experienced may, in some way, have contributed to where you are now. Or perhaps you went down a few dead ends in the process and got stuck. However, you arrived, and however long it has taken, you have surely travelled a long way emotionally and learnt a lot about yourself along the way. You may be able to see more objectively what your loved one meant to you, and what a deep wound their loss has caused, but most importantly, now you know that you have survived.

A popular contemporary phrase for constructing your life after bereavement is finding the 'new normal'. What does this phrase mean? At some point you may feel that life has become more normal, and that you are able to function, plan, socialise, and go about day-to-day business in ways you were just not able to do previously. That is not to say you are not still grieving, but just that the challenges of grief have lessened or you have grown accustomed to it and are able to cope better. Because the loss of your loved one has left an indelible mark on you, this is not 'normal' life as you knew it before, but rather a 'new' way to be normal. You are not exactly the same person you were previous to the loss; you may have new goals and a new outlook on life, perhaps more compassion for those who have also suffered loss, or become interested in causes that relate to your loved one or how they passed away. You would also have experienced a lot throughout your grief and have been through tough emotional times which are now part of your character. You may have had to readjust your habits and thoughts in reaction to your loss, in order to reach where you are now. For example, a song that you shared with your loved one when alive, which you couldn't bear to hear when grieving, now makes you both happy and nostalgic. You have learnt to experience the song in a new way, which will allow you to go on and establish your future.

You may feel you have reached some sort of summit, or at least a level plateau, but do not be surprised if every now and then you topple back into grief, as it is still very much part of who you still are. You will doubtless have good days and bad days, but on the whole, all the energy and time that was spent mourning and dealing with all the emotional challenges of grief can now be positively channelled into your future.

Although the acceptance of loss, or the 'resolution' of grief is in some ways the ultimate goal of the grieving process, it will never truly end there. Your loved one will live on in the memories and thoughts of those who were close to them, and there will always be strong emotions attached to them. Dr

Natasha Josefowitz, whose work we referred to earlier, identified the idea of post-grief as an emotional state to consider. In other words, that even after the grieving has largely ended, there may always be an ongoing sense of mourning in some form.

Making decisions for the long-term

There are many caveats to having an immediate or knee-jerk reaction to the loss of someone you love, such as deciding to move, quit your job, or enter into a new relationship. Time and time again, these rash, though understandable, decisions have hindered rather than helped the healing process, and you may find you will only have to go back again and unpick things to regain the focus on yourself. But as time goes on, and you feel that you have accepted the loss and are trying your best to move on, what kind of changes might you start to make? You may find that the loss of a spouse or a family has left a large gap in your life for a companion. Perhaps you could analyse whether getting a pet, such as a dog, would be a valuable and helpful progression for you? What would be the pros and cons? Another example would be moving closer to your support network if they are far away, perhaps a change of location and house may also help you adjust to your 'new normal' whilst also being closer to those who are there to help you in your grief. With every decision, talk it though with those around you and try to consider all the options. Most importantly, don't make any changes that will conceal your grief or try to deny the existence of your loved one. They should still be part of your life, whatever changes you now feel ready to make.

Example

Sometimes we have to choose options in life that we do not really want to accept, or maybe we have to choose ones that we would never have expected to arise. You may never have imagined having to live without your loved one, and perhaps have spent a long time in your grief fighting against the current reality and wishing for it not to be true. But accepting the situation that we are presented with is an important step to being able to move on and find a way to build a new future. Recently, there was a high profile example of this in the news, concerning Sheryl Sandberg, who is Chief Operating Officer of the huge social network site Facebook. She lost her husband, who was also a very well known online entrepreneur, in a tragic accident, and 30 days later she wrote a public post on her Facebook page to express her experience of grief and mourning thus far (6). Although it was very soon after the loss, she felt that she had only two options open to her, option A, which was having her husband, and option B, which was not having him. Of course, she wanted option A, but knew that all that really existed was option B. What lay before her was a struggle to accept it, and she writes:

"'Option A is not available. So let's just kick the s**t out of option B." Dave, to honor your memory and raise your children as they deserve to be raised, I promise to do all I can to kick the s**t out of option B.'

In this way, she is making a promise to herself and to her husband that she will embrace the reality of option B, one which she would never have wanted, but to do it for the sake of being able to move on with her and her family's life. She also adds poignantly: 'I still mourn for option A. I will always mourn for option A' and this is resonant with the idea of always having some form of grief – not necessarily negative – no matter how much time passes, or how much you rebuild you life.

Perhaps you can identify with this idea, and see what 'option B' you have in your life, and whether or not you are yet ready to try and accept it, even though, like Sheryl, you may always long, to some degree, for option A.

Key points to remember

- The acceptance of your loss can be seen as the key moment when you can really start to resolve the grieving process and begin to move on with your life, putting energy into your future.
- You may well find that you have changed, and establishing what is your 'new normal' is important in this new world that you find yourself in without your loved one.
- You may now feel yourself ready to start making long term decisions about your future, to readjust life without your loved one.
- Choosing life and forcing yourself to embrace the circumstances you have been given is crucial to surviving and moving on, though your loved one and your experience of grief will likely be an intricate part of you, and now defines who you now are.

Chapter 7
Self-help in dealing with grief

What is self-help?

We have already touched a little on some practical examples, as well as techniques such as cognitive behavioural therapy, which can help slowly build your pathway through grief and towards your recovery. In this chapter we want to focus on other ideas as to how you can help yourself – there are so many resources out there, scattered all over the internet and in books, and we want to bring together all the best ones in a concise and easy-to-understand way. Self-help is the idea that you can use methods and ideas to rely on yourself to get through difficult times, rather than having to only rely upon others, or remain inactive in your healing process. Essentially, being familiar with self-help techniques may help you build resilience, and relying on yourself can be the key to staying on track, and not getting lost in a fog of despair and hopelessness.

Of course, what is easy in theory is not always easy in practice, and when you are feeling tired and going through a difficult time in your grief, it isn't always simple to make yourself follow your own advice! But with luck, some of these ideas will resonate with you and there are enough to try from one day to the next, depending on how you feel.

Writing thoughts or keeping a journal

Writing can be extremely therapeutic. Some very good books on bereavement have been written by those while suffering it, and some even started out as personal journals, without the author having any intention of publishing their thoughts. Your journal entry can be written about how you feel, perhaps addressed to no-one in particular, or maybe you would see it as a chance to communicate with your loved one – perhaps an opportunity to tell them how much you miss them, or wish that you had said or done something differently when they were alive. With writing like this, there are no rules. You can write whatever, wherever and whenever you want. Some may like to buy a new and special book for these thoughts. Others may prefer loose bits of paper that they can throw in the bin or on the fire each night, to feel that they have exorcised those thoughts and feelings. However you go about it, it is your personal opportunity to express anything that might be inside your head at the moment, be it guilt, anger, or love. With no-one to judge you, you can be entirely free. You may like to re-read what you have written but try not to be too judgemental of yourself!

Some examples of entries could be:

- Sharing your thoughts with your loved one, what you did today, or passing on news from a mutual friend or family member.
- Confessing that you regret something or wish you'd behaved differently.
- Expressing how much you miss them or that something reminded you of them today.
- Asking yourself why you felt so angry or sad at the moment.
- Writing down a favourite memory and how it makes you feel to recall it.

- Writing down your hopes for the short-term, perhaps that soon you hope to feel better and return to work.

Creating a weekly plan

Planning ahead can help you set tasks for yourself day by day and week by week, the overall goal being to keep active, sociable, and to be able to release your grief and associated emotions through different channels – be they physical, the distraction of entertainment, or through the mental exertions of learning something new. By dividing up the week into days, and by splitting days into morning, afternoon and evening, you can make it more likely that you will pass the time in a positive way, and avoid becoming bored or isolated. It can be helpful to have a guide to refer to for when you feel lost or disillusioned, and may assist keeping you on track and looking after yourself.

Firstly, make a list of things that you previously enjoyed doing regularly, such as –

- Going to the cinema or theatre.
- Having lunch, dinner, or just a brief coffee with a friend.
- Walking through a local park, or taking a swim.
- Communicating with friends or family members whom you don't see regularly, and allocating time to call or write an email to them.

Then you can add new ideas to your list, such as things that you would like to do or try – something creative perhaps, like a photography class, pottery, cooking, or anything else that grabs your interest. Notice boards at local libraries and shopping centres, and even the local paper, can often advertise what's on and where.

Lastly, add treats for yourself, such as buying something nice, buying tickets to a sporting match or spectacle, having a massage or a haircut, buying some exotic foods or treating yourself in an expensive café.

Then take these lists and use them to make yourself a plan for the week ahead, inserting as many activities or ideas as you think reasonable throughout the week. Try to be realistic and do not over challenge yourself, otherwise you may just bring on an unnecessary sense of failure if you do not manage everything you have planned.

Once you have made the plan, try to follow it day by day – allow yourself to be flexible, but try not to let yourself give up on everything. A major set-back will only hurt you in the long run, so try to avoid that happening. Similarly, don't dwell on days that you didn't do anything, or tore up the plan, as that is behind you. Try to look forward to what you can do, what you are capable of doing. After all, it's up to you.

Keeping healthy

Many people appreciate that there is a strong relationship between mind and body. If you keep your body healthy and active, you are more likely to have more positive thoughts and feelings. Because of this, keeping a varied and balanced diet is important. Feeling sluggish and undernourished will only make finding energy and motivation to do anything even harder. Reaching for quick fixes like junk food, alcohol, or even drugs, for a low or negative mood, will be counterproductive in the long term, and will not keep our bodies or minds healthy.

As we have touched on before, physical exercise is also very beneficial and there is always something that you can find to do, whether walking, running, gardening or something more demanding such as rock climbing, racquet sports or gym classes. Incorporate physical fitness into your weekly plan and try to keep to as much as possible, or at least replace an activity that you no longer want to do, with something else less challenging.

Getting out and about

Of course, there may be times when you just don't want social interaction and feel that the world is alien and an unfamiliar place. But you might be surprised how many people you meet will be able to instantly empathise and understand your grief, as the death of a loved one is something that surely affects us all at some point in our life. No one can fully comprehend your personal experience, but they may well identify with your position and offer you advice or bits of wisdom that have been supportive to their journey. That is not to say everyone will be helpful – there may well be someone who glosses over your loss and is insensitive, or someone that ignores you because they don't know what to say. There will always be someone who is uneasy in this situation and won't be helpful, but more often than not, social interaction will be supportive and positive.

If you find that your social network isn't as strong as it once was, then make attempts to build new ones. Voluntary work for local charities can be a very good way to meet new people, as well as joining local groups such as book clubs or various hobby interest groups. It is daunting for anyone at the best of times to meet new people, and you may be feeling shaky on confidence, but now is the time to give it a try.

Online networks

Like getting out and about, making new friends online can also be an excellent way to share stories and experiences, as well as build a new horizon for yourself. The internet is awash with communities, forums and websites specific to common interests or experiences, and with just a few clicks, you can find yourself welcomed into a world where like-minded people understand your situation, and can respond to anything you say without all the judgements and issues that come along with knowing you well. It is a different way to interact and isn't for everybody, but if you are seeking new ways to deal with your grief and people to share it with, then this could be an opportunity.

Making a lasting memorial

It can help the grieving process to throw your energy into a new project – and what better project is there than building a lasting memorial to your loved one? A memorial could be either something physical, such as a memory garden where you can plant flowers or even a tree in honour of the one who has died. If you have lots of pictures and video clips of the person, you could consider making a memorial film that celebrates their life and that you can share with others, or keep only for you when you want to be reminded of them. Some people like to accumulate special items that relate to their loved one such as items of clothing, favourite books, or their reading glasses, and put them together in a memory box. An engraved stone or bench dedicated in their memory are other popular ideas.

Some people like to create an online memorial, such as a dedicated webpage or blog, where they can put photos and celebrate the life of their loved one. It can also be a good opportunity to write about their feelings and share their bereavement journey too, if they so choose. Also popular is creating a memorial page on Facebook to which a group of friends and family can post comments and pictures. This is a really easy way to gather and share thoughts and memories, and something that can grow continually with everyone's input.

Some throw themselves into wider causes, either inspired by a cause related to their loved one, or perhaps how they passed away, perhaps setting up a foundation in their memory or becoming involved in charity work.

Key points to remember

- Self-help ideas are tools to use in order to manage all the challenges you may face in a practical way.

- You can interpret all the ideas in a way that makes them appropriate and personal to you and your experience.
- Being self-reliant is the key to helping you resolve the grieving process in a way that helps you find your feet and build your future.

Chapter 8
When to seek help for unresolved grief

Unresolved or 'complicated' grief

The strong emotional states written about above will likely impair your life to some degree after bereavement, and it is normal that at times, your grief may almost define your existence and sometimes prevent you from doing other things. But when does grief become abnormal and a serious problem? Some may find themselves stuck at some point in the grieving process, whether in anger, depression, or a mixture of all this and more, and not know how to help themselves out of it. Getting trapped in a cycle of negative feelings and evasive behaviour can mean you risk becoming isolated, and it may be a longer and more painful journey before you can begin to resolve your grief. This is what people call 'complicated' grief, a form of grief that has taken you over and just won't let go.

So – how do you know you might need help? As with everything there is no hard and fast rule, it is just keeping a measure of yourself and trying to recognise when you are becoming a little lost in the grieving process. Here are some signs:

- Constantly avoiding people or places that remind you of the person.
- Seeking to avoid any social interaction at all, such as ignoring phone calls or knocks at the door.
- Avoiding dates and festive celebrations.
- Feeling that your life is meaningless and that you will never be happy again.
- Continually fantasising that the person is still alive, or refusing to acknowledge their passing.
- A depressive period that has lasted a couple of weeks or more where you have lost all interest or pleasure in life.
- Severe unresolved issues with the death, such as unrealistic guilt or anger, which have begun to impair your normal life.
- You feel yourself just unable to move on with life, even if considerable time has passed since you were bereaved.

What are the 'risk factors' that can make grief more complicated to resolve? Here are some factors that can make bereavement even more of a testing time, and can, in some cases, cause grief to become an issue that needs professional help:

- The person was very close to you and part of your daily life.
- The person helped define your life or identity, such as a spouse or parent.
- Having other problems in your life such as financial problems and relationship issues.
- Not having an adequate support network.
- Experiencing multiple losses all in one go or close together.
- The death being very sudden or completely unexpected.
- The circumstances of the death, e.g. an event that causes ensuing court cases and publicity, or an incident deemed to be the fault of someone else.

Seeking support

You may find that you are trying to talk yourself out of getting help, telling yourself that you will get better with time, that counselling won't work, maybe the problems will go away on their own, or perhaps you are in denial that you have a problem at all. Maybe someone close to you suggested you get help, and you reacted angrily? Finally recognising that perhaps you need to seek some professional or outside help to assist you with your grief is the first important step. There are many support options and resources available to you and you will surely be able to find the right help to address your needs.

Your GP can refer you to a counsellor to help talk through the issues you are experiencing, or you may wish to find your own private counsellor − for which you can refer to http://www.bacp.co.uk/ to find a list of accredited ones in your area. The NHS website has an online search for bereavement support groups that you can join locally, as do many charities, set up to address specific bereavement types, such as loss of a child or bereavement by suicide. Some national charities such as Cruse offer general bereavement support either over the telephone or via email.

Useful links to support resources

http://www.nhs.uk/Service-Search/Bereavement-information-and-support-services/LocationSearch/314
http://www.cruse.org.uk/
http://www.macmillan.org.uk/in-your-area/choose-location.html
http://www.childbereavementuk.org/support/
http://www.tcf.org.uk/
http://uk-sobs.org.uk/support-group/
http://www.samaritans.org/

Key points to remember

- Try to check yourself for warning signs that your grief is becoming 'complicated' and that you're risking becoming lost or stuck in the process.
- Some factors may influence your response to bereavement and make it more likely that you will have a harder time getting through it, such as the length of time you know the person and how close they were to you, together with personal issues such as financial problems or a poor support network.
- There are many support groups organised who would welcome your participation and may be able to give you more of the assistance that you need to deal with your grief.
- Some people turn to counselling and therapy if they feel that they need extra help, and can do so either through their GP or through seeking their own counselling professional.

Conclusions

Bereavement and grief

Just as dying is an inevitable part of the life cycle, experiencing grief after bereavement is also intrinsic to being alive, and part and parcel of loving those around you. When you lose someone precious to you, the degree of love you once felt can be reflected in the degree of pain you experience now that they are gone. Happy memories become agony, and you may find it difficult to imagine that you can survive. Not only do you mourn for your loved one, you mourn for yourself; you used to be so happy and carefree, and everything was better. Now a cloud of strong emotions – such as those we have talked about above – may be enveloping you and you may feel powerless and lost from one day to the next. The important thing to remember is that what you are experiencing is a normal reaction to the intensely challenging and potentially life-changing event that has occurred. You may emerge from the process bruised and battered, but you will surely survive.

Grief is a universal experience with some common factors, though everyone deals with a loss differently, and what helps one person may not be helpful to another. The examples and ideas we have covered in the book are meant solely as a reference and to provoke thought and insight into some of the emotions that bereavement can ignite. Two things stand out as important factors in helping resolving your grief and these are:

- Support: having a strong, diverse, and flexible social network of people around you who can listen, care for you, and if appropriate, give advice when you need it.
- Self-reliance: attempting to understand your emotions and experiences, and using self-help

techniques and practical ideas to remain proactive throughout the grieving process.

Letting go of your grief and untangling yourself from the web of powerful emotions will not mean that you lose closeness or proximity to your loved one; they will remain eternally in your thoughts and memories, as well as in those of other people. Try to foster a continued bond with the dead loved one, through building living memories of them in memorials you make, causes you support in their name, or just in your daily life by mentioning them in conversation or acknowledging them by marking special dates and places. Don't feel guilty for trying to heal, and give yourself permission to move forward in your life. Consider what your loved one would wish for you, and you would likely conclude that they would want you to move on.

Remember that you can recover a true sense of happiness and purpose even if life may be forever different to how it was before, or how you'd planned. There is no shame in grieving and mourning for as long as you want to, until you are ready to accept your loss, and move on with appreciating your life for everything that you have.

Further reading

<u>A Grief Observed</u> by C.S. Lewis
The great author writes an illuminating personal account of grief following the death of his wife, exploring innermost thoughts and feelings as well as the impact of the loss on his Christianity.

<u>Death... And How To Survive It: A Unique, Practical and Uplifting Guide to Coming to Terms with the Loss of Your Partner</u> by Kate Bodell
A practical and very reader friendly guide on how to come to terms to the loss of someone (in this case her partner).

<u>Living On The Seabed: A Memoir of Love, Life and Survival</u> by Lindsay Nicholson
An articulate and emotional account of loss and how to rebuild your life. The author lost her husband and daughter to leukaemia and tells her story in an honest and powerful way that gives many relevant tips about how to appreciate your life even without your loved ones.

<u>'You'll Get Over It': The Rage of Bereavement</u> by Virginia Ironside
A helpful reference book for those dealing with bereavement, in particular confronting the anger issues and finding a way through difficult social interaction.

<u>Courage to Grieve: Creative Living, Recovery and Growth Through Grief</u> by Judy Tatelbaum
Full of helpful and practical advice, it is a popular reference for people wishing to understand and resolve their grief

<u>Overcoming Grief</u> by Sue Morris
This is a self-help guide to the grieving process, full of cognitive behavioural techniques and ideas.

References

1) Kubler-Ross, E (1969). *On Death and Dying*, Routledge
2) Prigerson, H.G. & Maciejewski, P.K. (2008). 'Grief and acceptance as opposite sides of the same coin: setting a research agenda to study peaceful acceptance of loss.' The British Journal of Psychiatry Nov 2008, 193 (6) 435-437
3) Josefowitz, N. (2014).'A New Look at the 7 Emotional States of Loss' [online]. Huffington Post. Available from: http://www.huffingtonpost.com/dr-natasha-josefowitz/loss-grief_b_5556644.html [Accessed June 2015]
4) Maciejewski P.K., Zhang B., Block S.D., Prigerson H.G. (2007). 'An empirical examination of the stage theory of grief.' JAMA 2007 Feb 21;297(7):716-23
5) McCarthy, M.R. (2002). 'Gender differences in reactions to perinatal loss: A qualitative study of couples.' Dissertation Abstracts International: Section B: the Sciences & Engineering. 62(8-B), March, 3809
6) Sandberg, S. (2015). Facebook. Available from: https://www.facebook.com/sheryl/posts/10155617891025177:0 [Accessed June 2015]